IMAGES
of America

US COAST GUARD
TRAINING CENTER
AT CAPE MAY

Taken about 1970, this official US Coast Guard photograph shows the location of the training center in Cape May, New Jersey. The site is bordered by the Atlantic Ocean to the south, Cape May Inlet and Canal to the east, and Cape May Harbor (in the foreground) to the north, making it ideal for open water exercises. (Courtesy of the US Coast Guard.)

ON THE COVER: The CG-100s were 75-foot patrol boats built specifically for Prohibition enforcement duties. Known as "six-bitters," they entered US Coast Guard service between 1924 and 1925 and a total of 203 were constructed. They had a top speed of 15 knots, slower than most of the rumrunners they were up against, but they were known as sturdy, well-built craft capable of offshore operations. (Courtesy of the Naval Air Station Wildwood Aviation Museum.)

IMAGES
of America

US COAST GUARD
TRAINING CENTER
AT CAPE MAY

Joseph E. Salvatore, MD, and Joan Berkey

ARCADIA
PUBLISHING

Published by Arcadia Publishing
Charleston, South Carolina

Printed in the United States of America

Library of Congress Control Number: 2012941983

For all general information, please contact Arcadia Publishing:
Telephone 843-853-2070
Fax 843-853-0044
E-mail sales@arcadiapublishing.com
For customer service and orders:
Toll-Free 1-888-313-2665

Visit us on the Internet at www.arcadiapublishing.com

To the men and women who have served or trained here since 1917

CONTENTS

ACKNOWLEDGMENTS

The authors wish to thank H. Gerald MacDonald, Andi Thomas, Tom Carroll, Mike O'Rourke, Clay Sutton, Capt. Charles Meyer, Liz Bendix, John Fitzgerald, Comdr. Gary Thomas, USCG (Ret.), Annie Salvatore, the Cape May County Historical and Genealogy Society, the Wildwood Historical Society, the Greater Cape May Historical Society, the Mid-Atlantic Center for the Arts and Humanities, the Howell Family, and the US Coast Guard Training Center. We also thank Ken Freeze for his online story and for sharing photographs of famous Coast Guard aviator Charles Thrun.

All of these people have contributed knowledge and resources in support of this book. Also deserving of a big thank you is our Arcadia editor, Abby Henry, who kindly shepherded us through the whole process from start to finish.

Unless otherwise noted, photographs and images are from the archives of the Naval Air Station Wildwood Aviation Museum, many of them generously donated by H. Gerald MacDonald.

INTRODUCTION

In April 1917, the federal government established US Navy Section Base Nine on several hundred acres approximately three miles east of the city of Cape May in Cape May County, New Jersey. The location of the Cape May base was strategic. Situated midway between New York harbor and the Virginia Capes, it guards the mouth of the Delaware River, which is the only navigable waterway to the United States Navy Yard and defense industries in Philadelphia.

The site where the base was built, known as Sewell's Point, was named for Civil War veteran and railroad director Gen. William J. Sewell, who developed the area in the 1860s. He established a horse trolley line from Cape May to the point, where he built a restaurant for summer vacationers. In the 1880s, a steam locomotive took visitors to his hotel and yacht pier. An amusement park known as the Fun Factory was built at the site in 1913 and Cape May's popular boardwalk was then extended to Sewell's Point.

Part of the amusement park—a fun house and skating rink—was adapted for military use when the section base was established. The amusement park had been abandoned for two years and its buildings were vacant. An airfield and a 66-foot-tall hangar were also built to accommodate dirigibles, which were just coming into use for reconnaissance. Also erected on the base were a firing range and several other structures, the majority of which burned to the ground on July 4, 1918. A new, larger base was immediately rebuilt on the site.

By November 1918, the base contained 12 seaplanes, one dirigible, and one kite balloon. During World War I, the base provided operational support to minesweepers and submarine chasers that were being developed as anti-submarine weapons. The dirigible hangar was doubled in size in 1920 to house an English-built dirigible; however, the airship crashed into the English Channel during its trial trip and the hangar was never used for its original purpose. By 1920, the Coast Guard and the Navy were jointly using the base. With the increase in rumrunners plying the coast during Prohibition, the Coast Guard took over the site almost entirely in 1926. It was used for enforcing Prohibition laws.

In 1926, the Cape May Coast Guard air station opened as an adjunct to Section Base Nine. Located adjacent to the base, it had a fleet of amphibian biplanes that was later replaced by amphibious airplanes nicknamed "flying lifeboats." Several noteworthy aviators were stationed here, among them Navy lieutenant commander Elmer F. Stone and lieutenant Richard Burke. Stone was one of the pilots on the first transatlantic flight in 1919, while Burke set several national and international speed records in 1935.

The Coast Guard abandoned Section Base Nine in 1934, but the air station remained in operation and was used by the Navy Reserves, along with part of the patrol fleet. In 1937, the US Marine Corps occupied the base briefly, holding Officers Training School there during the summer. However, the Navy retained title to the land and established Naval Air Station Cape May on the site in September 1940. Buildings were added and renovated, piers were reconstructed, and the roads and grounds were improved. At first, a "Neutrality Patrol Unit" operated from the air station, using 12 scouting seaplanes and one blimp. The original dirigible hangar was deteriorated, and because it also obscured the view of the airfield from the control tower being built, it was demolished in 1941. After that time, the Cape May airfield was used as an auxiliary station for blimps operating out of Naval Air Station Lakehurst about 60 miles to the north.

As the threat from German U-boats along the coastline increased before the United States entered World War II, the importance of Naval Air Station Cape May's ability to patrol and monitor submarine activity off the coast became apparent. Located on the Atlantic coastline just a few miles north of the mouth of the Delaware River and the bay, the base was strategically located for coastal defense. It also abutted Cape May Sound, which provided a protected harbor for its vessels. An Inshore Patrol Squadron comprised of subchasers, cutters, Navy utility vessels, and several minesweepers was established there, as was an antisubmarine warfare school.

The importance of the base's air station waned as Naval Air Station Wildwood, built in 1942 a few miles to the northwest, was established for the training of dive-bombers during World War II. However, the Cape May air station remained home to an experimental Navy flight squadron that conducted highly classified work on aircraft radar, communications, and antiaircraft defenses. There was also a permanent scouting patrol squadron that provided cover for convoys.

In 1944, at the height of the war, the air station had 36 aircraft and facilities for two blimps, 151 officers, 1,050 enlisted men, and 138 civilian personnel. That same year, the Coast Guard had an Air Sea Rescue Unit based at the station.

In June 1946, the Coast Guard took over the base with the stated purpose of using it as a "headquarters for surface craft, air craft, the buoy service and other Coast Guard activities designed to promote the safety of boatmen and seafarers in the Cape May sector."

In 1948, the Coast Guard recruit-training base at the naval air station in Mayport, Florida, was closed and relocated to Cape May. In 1982, the Cape May location became the sole recruit-training center when another training center in Alameda, California, was closed. The site is still used for that purpose, graduating approximately 4,000 recruits per year on an almost weekly basis.

Very few World War I and World War II buildings remain, but those that do, like the commanding officer's quarters, continue to serve a useful function. Over 350 military and civilian personnel are attached to the training center. In addition to boot camp, the Direct Entry Petty Officer Training Course, the Company Commander School, and the four-week Recruiter School are also conducted here. Sunset parades, held three times each summer, are open to the public and feature the recruit band, the drill team, and marching troops.

One

THE EARLY YEARS

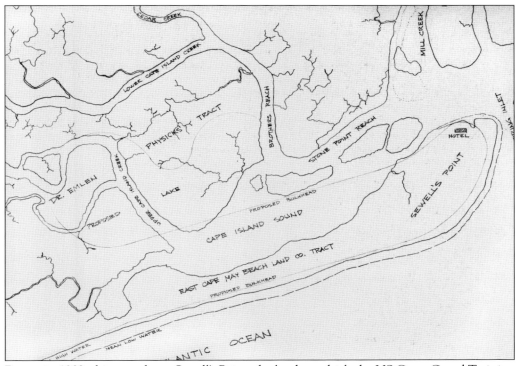

Drawn in 1902, this map shows Sewell's Point, the land on which the US Coast Guard Training Center was eventually built. Located about three miles east of Cape May, Sewell's Point was named for Civil War veteran and railroad director Gen. William Sewell, who developed the area for summer vacationers in the 1860s. In the 1880s, the point had a hotel and a pier, which were reached by train.

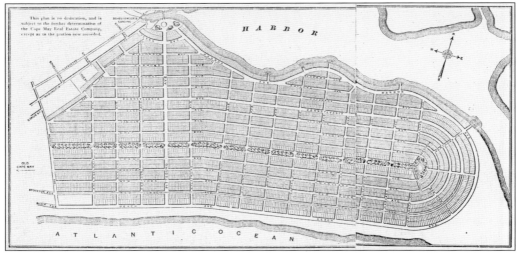

Hoping to capitalize on Cape May's popularity as a seaside resort, the Cape May Land Company bought the large Sewell's Point tract, created new streets, and subdivided it in the early 1900s into 7,500 building lots, which averaged 60 feet wide and 125 feet deep. Only a few cottages were built and the development faltered after a few years.

In 1913, a new developer built the Fun Factory amusement park at the eastern tip of Sewell's Point. It featured a carousel, a revolving barrel, and a large slide that people rode while sitting on a piece of burlap. Trolleys from Cape May made stops at the site every 10 minutes and charged 15¢ for a round trip. The Fun Factory closed in 1915.

Part of the vacant amusement park—the fun house and skating rink—was adapted for military use when US Navy Section Base Nine was established on Sewell's Point in April 1917. At the time, it was the best available site in Cape May for a new section base. This tower was originally part of the amusement park and featured a viewing platform at the top that was 85 feet above the water. Four feet of wind-blown sand had to be cleared from the floor of the abandoned skating rink when it was converted into the mess hall and sleeping quarters. The stage was converted into a galley.

In a novel reuse of existing structures, the Fun Factory's revolving barrel was converted into the section base brig. The trolley line, which originally transported vacationers from Cape May to Sewell's Point, was bought by the federal government. One hundred US Navy reservists reconditioned the abandoned line and placed two storage-battery trolley cars into service, eliminating the need for overhead wires. Also put into service was a small gasoline locomotive (below), which was used to transport freight cars to and from the naval base. It was also used to pull streetcars like this one, full of Navy men on leave, between the barracks and Cape May, earning it the name "Liberty Special."

The Corinthian Yacht Club, built in 1913, was requisitioned by the US government for use as Section Base Nine headquarters in 1918. It overlooked the harbor and stood across from the present quarters of the Coast Guard base commander. The building featured social rooms, a dining room, and many upstairs bedrooms when used by the yacht club. (Courtesy of the Wildwood Historical Society.)

Three unnamed Navy officers pose in front of the Corinthian Club headquarters building in this undated photograph. Two are naval commanders and one is a lieutenant junior grade. Behind them are members of the band, likely the 28 men who reported for duty on July 1, 1917, as musicians. (Courtesy of the Wildwood Historical Society.)

Edward L. Bader, a building contractor based in Atlantic City, built the first pier at the section base. The pile-driving crane is seen here on a barge in the water. It was likely fired by gas. Bader later served as mayor of Atlantic City, and that city's now-vacant airport, Bader Field, was named for him.

US Navy men use pulleys to raise and lower the targets at the rifle range around 1918. The range was built at a cost of $8,500, and because fresh water was not available, the range was constructed of concrete mixed with salt water. By the spring of 1919, more than three million rounds of ammunition for rifle, revolver, and pistol practice had been used.

CAMP WISSAHICKON, U. S. NAVAL TRAINING STATION.   CAPE MAY, N. J.
Entrance.

Camp Wissahickon was built in 1917 across from Sewell's Point as a Navy Reserve training center for 3,000 men. The camp, located near where the Garden State Parkway ends today, was constructed at a cost of $1.5 million, with the city of Cape May furnishing water and sewer lines without charge. The camp was abandoned after 1919.

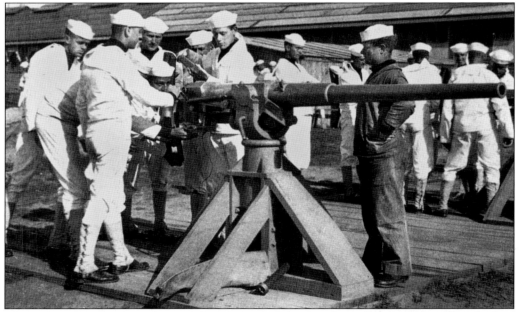

These Navy reservists in white uniforms train on three-inch artillery at Camp Wissahickon while a regular Navy man dressed in blue directs them in 1918. In addition to practice aiming and shooting guns, the reservists also received instruction in seamanship, knot-tying, signals with semaphores and wig-wag flags, boating, and marching.

Training at Camp Wissahickon was rigorous. Because most of the Navy ships were sailing vessels, it was imperative that the reservists learned how to climb the masts, raise and lower sails, and hone their balancing skills. The camp featured this large mast, a replica of the masts reservists would encounter on real ships.

MAST DRILL — "OVER THE TOP".

Camp Wissachickon was constructed on a farm leased by the government from Henry Ford. Construction began in July 1917, with 400 carpenters and 200 assistants erecting mostly one-story buildings. Ford was considering bringing an automobile factory and test track to the county as early as 1908, but he eventually abandoned the plan. The barracks are seen here in 1918.

PHYSICAL DRILL UNDER ARMS.

The level, open land of Henry Ford's farm provided plenty of space to conduct drills for Navy reservists at Camp Wissahickon. When the camp was dismantled in 1919, materials from structures like these were used for new construction in Cape May and its environs. One building was moved to nearby Cold Spring, where it was used as a speakeasy.

The mess hall at Camp Wissahickon, seen here in 1918, had several entrances to accommodate the rush of hungry reservists. A pipe carrying steam heat into the building and supported by posts is seen to the left. The training mast is behind the building. The hydrant was needed in case any of the highly flammable wooden structures caught fire.

On July 5, 1918, all of the men stationed at the section base were on parade in Cape May when word was received that the base was on fire. Navy men rode back in any vehicle available but were unable to save the barracks and its distinctive two-story tower. The powder magazine and gun range were spared, however. An early newspaper account deemed the fire suspicious, and although witnesses saw the fire erupt simultaneously in four places, no proof of sabotage was ever proven. Personnel lost all of their personal possessions and more than $200,000 of naval equipment was destroyed.

After the devastating fire, most of the 600 Navy men were billeted in tents that lined Pennsylvania Avenue, the main road into and out of the section base. Thankfully, the summer weather made camping out more enjoyable than if the fire had occurred in the winter. However, Cape May's notoriously large mosquitoes were probably less than enjoyable. (Courtesy of the Wildwood Historical Society.)

Temporary buildings, like the wood-framed, one-story YMCA, sprung up to accommodate the men's needs. A group of tents placed together sheltered rows of picnic-style tables that served as the mess hall. The sailors were forced to wear donated street clothing for several weeks until their Navy-issued uniforms could be replaced. (Courtesy of the Wildwood Historical Society.)

The US Navy rebuilt Section Base Nine after the fire and, in less than nine months, had erected the fully functioning base and air station seen here in April 1919. Most building supplies were brought in by rail on the tracks of the trolley line. The largest of the new buildings was the dirigible hangar, at right. The hangar was erected to house the "lighter than air" airships that debuted as weapons in World War I. Two other hangars, to the left, accommodated seaplanes and had ramps into the harbor. At least six twin-engine flying boats are parked near them. Other new buildings included a mess hall, men's and officer's quarters, and an infirmary. The Navy's first successful dirigible, the B-1, completed its first overnight test flight in May 1917, the same month that the Navy established an 18-month course to qualify officers as pilots of either seaplanes or dirigibles. At the signing of the armistice in November 1918, the Navy owned 15 dirigibles.

This photograph, taken on January 30, 1919, shows how railroad cars were loaded with building materials and brought to the site on the old trolley tracks. The tall smokestack near the center of the image marks the location of the new power plant. The two-story barracks and officer's quarters for the air station are also seen here.

The new commanding officer's quarters is seen here under construction in 1918. Its American Four Square style, complete with a fireplace in the living room and a wide front porch, was an immensely popular residential style at the time. The house has been renovated several times over the years but still stands at its original location.

Built adjacent to each other, these two hangars were constructed to shelter seaplanes, many of them bi-wing, used by the Navy at the time. These hangars were used to service the seaplanes attached to the Navy airfield at the east end of the base. Each had its own separate group of buildings and departments.

The Navy air station at the base's east end had its own cluster of buildings. In this 1919 photograph, a seaplane hangar is to the right and an unidentified building is under construction to the left. A group of men watch a Curtiss R-6 utility plane, a model produced for the US Army and Navy during World War I, take off from the shoreline.

During World War I, submarine patrols were also part of the duties on Section Base Nine, particularly with the threat of attack from German U-boats along the coast. The Cape May base was strategically sited at the mouth of the Delaware River, the only navigable waterway to the US Navy Yard and the defense industries in Philadelphia. In this 1919 photograph, five O-series submarines and their sub-tender, the USS *Savannah*, are docked in Cape May. Many of the N- and O-series submarines were built just prior to the United States's entry into World War I, and some, like the O-14 seen here, were commissioned too late to serve in the war. These 175-foot-long submarines were built by the California Shipbuilding Company in Long Beach, California. O-14 reported to Cape May in 1919, was decommissioned in 1924, and was scrapped in 1930. More like submersible ships than the submarines of today, these vessels operated primarily on the surface using standard engines, submerging only occasionally to attack under battery power.

The C-3 dirigible is tethered outside of the US Navy Section Base Nine's dirigible hangar in the fall of 1918. Sporting the French colors of red, white, and blue on its rudder, the C-3 was the first lighter-than-air ship to fly at Cape May and was one of 10 C-type blimps developed for patrol by the Navy shortly after World War I. All 10 were delivered in late 1918 and served at all of

the Navy's airship stations in 1919 and 1920. They were used for training, for tracking practice torpedoes fired from submarines, and for releasing airplanes while in flight. Capable of reaching a maximum speed of 60 miles per hour, they were 196 feet long, 42 feet in diameter, 54 feet high, and were manned by a crew of four.

This close-up photograph of the C-3 dirigible shows three of the crewmen in the blimp's gondola, or control car. The car was built by the Burgess division of Curtiss Aeroplane and Motor Company, the largest American aircraft manufacturer in the 1920s and 1930s. The dirigible's envelope was made by either Goodyear or Goodrich, as both companies produced them.

Seen here around 1919 with the section base barracks in the background, the C-3 dirigible established the world's endurance record for nonrigid blimps on February 18, 1919, when it remained aloft for 33 hours and six minutes despite snow, high winds, and extremely low temperatures. The C-3 was also used to raise money for the Victory Liberty Loan campaign. (Courtesy of the Mid-Atlantic Center for the Arts and Humanities.)

US Navy men, one of whom is holding a trombone, watch as two others examine part of a single-engine plane on a muddied dirt road near the dirigible hangar around 1919. The three-cylinder engine is likely a Lawrance L-3, which was used by the Navy to power its SA-1 and Loening M-2 Kitten aircraft. (Courtesy of the Wildwood Historical Society.)

This 1919 aerial photograph shows the USS *Savannah* docked at one of the section base's piers. The *Savannah* was a 10,800-ton submarine tender built in Germany in 1899 as a commercial freighter. Seized by the United States in April 1917, it was turned over to the US Navy, converted for submarine support purposes, and commissioned in early November 1917.

The dirigible hangar was more than doubled in size in the spring of 1920 to accommodate the gigantic blimp ZR-2. Using both new materials and parts from a dismantled 250-foot hangar from Montauk, on Long Island, the new hangar was built by 300 men and was expanded to be 107 feet high, 708 feet long, and 133 feet wide. Seen here in 1929, it had a steel frame with steel windows and doors, corrugated siding, composition flooring, and concrete footings. The English-built ZR-2 was originally intended for long-range patrol duties over the North Sea by Britain's Royal Navy. The US Navy purchased it in 1919 for $2 million, but it never made it to the states, crashing from structural failure during a trial run in England on August 23, 1921. When built, the hangar at Cape May was the largest in the world at the time.

This early-1920s aerial view shows the enormity of the new dirigible hangar at the east end of the naval base. Behind it are the four airways that served the Cape May Air Station. Several boats are docked along the waterfront. Note the two water towers, which are both painted with a checkerboard design to avoid being struck by aircraft.

The interior of the new hangar, seen here in the 1930s, shows the elaborate structural steel framework that supported the hangar's sides and arched roof. Cars, probably used by base officers and staff, line one side of the hangar. Two North American O-47 airplanes are on the right and a crew of three sits in tandem under the long canopy. Windows in the deep belly allowed downward observation and photography.

This 1920s photograph shows the expanded hangar in the background, its giant size dwarfing the buildings in the foreground. Two Navy men on the right appear to be scavenging for building materials in a scrap yard filled with piles of wood and leftover metal, which was near the edge of the harbor.

A wood-plank catwalk, seen here in the 1920s or 1930s, traversed the full 708-foot length of the newly expanded hangar. A clerestory of steel windows provided much-needed light. The structural steel beams supporting the roof structure are held with immense rivets. An observation booth was located at the north end of the building.

Two

PROHIBITION
AND THE 1930S

In 1926, the US Coast Guard acquired the Cape May facility and the site became the first permanent Coast Guard Air Station. It was equipped with one seaplane and one amphibian aircraft, both of which were used for rescue and antismuggling operations. By the fall of that year, the air station had three amphibious biplanes housed in the former Navy blimp hangar, visible in the background of this photograph.

Prohibition went into effect in January 1920, and within a year, the US Coast Guard found itself in an all-out war with those smuggling illegal liquor into the country. One of the rumrunner's favorite spots was the Jersey coast, not only because of its many inlets and miles of deserted beaches but also because of the speakeasies serving thirsty patrons in the many shore resorts. Beginning in the mid-1920s, Cape May was home to 75-foot patrol boats used to help chase down illegal liquor traffickers in southern New Jersey. In this 1926 postcard are four patrol boats, known as "six-bitters," which were built in 1924–1925 by Mathis Yacht Company and stationed at Cape May. One of the largest seizures off of Cape May was in 1925, when $100,000 worth of whiskey, champagne, and cordials packed in 800 cases were found on the *Kingfisher*—ironically a former sub-chaser converted into a rumrunner. Bathers along the seashore also reported seeing gun battles between Coast Guard patrols and rum boats.

The 157-foot *Kickapoo*, built by Bethlehem Steel in 1919, is seen here in the mid-1920s. Originally the seagoing tug *Baldridge*, it was taken over by the Coast Guard, reconditioned as a cruising cutter, and renamed on November 9, 1921. It was first assigned to duty at Cape May, where it intercepted several rumrunners. On January 2, 1925, it rescued the entire crew and all 227 passengers on the American steamer *Mohawk* at Brandywine Shoals, Delaware, landing them safely at Lewes, Delaware. In 1926, *Kickapoo* was modified for light icebreaking and its hull was widened by 8.5 feet. It was transferred to Rockland, Maine, where it served as an icebreaker. During World War II, it was classified as a buoy tender and given the hull number and designation WAGL-56. It was assigned to Buzzard's Bay, Massachusetts, where it continued to serve as an icebreaker and also carried out general aids to navigation duties. *Kickapoo* was decommissioned in August 1945.

Several vessels are tied up at the coaling pier during the mid-1920s. It was not uncommon for private boats to use the piers at the base. Records show that as late as the early 1940s, private boat owners would tie up at the pier seeking remedy for both medical and mechanical emergencies.

Cracked from age, this black and white photograph shows the expanded dirigible hangar in 1926. The hangar was on the east side of the base and was part of the air station. Shown in the foreground is the pipe for the steam-heating system, supported on metal posts.

The US Coast Guard also operated the Two Mile Beach Life Saving Station on the opposite side of Cold Spring Inlet, not far from the Coast Guard base and air station. Seen above in the early 1920s, the building was eventually razed, and in 1947, the Coast Guard opened its Long Range Navigation, or LORAN, system there. Later, the Coast Guard Electronic Engineering Center (EECEN) was built nearby on the site. In 1923, the wood-framed building below housed a crew of nine—a boatswain, his mate, and seven surfmen. A station at this location was authorized in 1854 and is believed to have been discontinued in 1925.

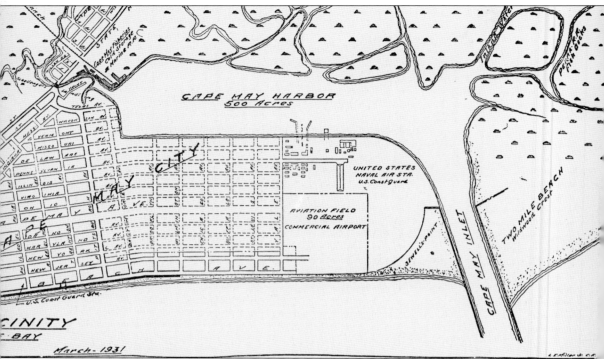

This 1931 map identifies the site as the "United States Naval Air Station and U.S. Coast Guard." At the time, the air station was under the control of the Coast Guard, which had commissioned Air Station Cape May in 1926 under the command of Carl C. Von Paulsen. Cape May Air Station was originally equipped with one seaplane and one amphibian aircraft, both of which were used for rescue and antismuggling operations. The various types of aircraft that flew out of Air Station Cape May were hangared in the former Navy blimp hanger or the seaplane hangar and launched into the harbor on a wooden ramp. In the late 1920s, the future of Cape May as a Coast Guard air base seemed uncertain, and for a time it appeared likely to be abandoned to commercial aviation, either as an airport or as a flight school. For a short period of time, from 1929 to 1934, part of the base was used as a civilian airport.

Elmer "Archie" Stone (1887–1936), who signed this photograph, reported as the commanding officer of Cape May US Coast Guard Air Station on March 8, 1932, serving there until 1934. Stone was a Coast Guard aviation pioneer and, with officer Norman B. Hall, was the first to suggest that the Coast Guard develop an aviation capability. He became the Coast Guard's first aviator in 1917, and in 1919, he was the pilot on the first successful transatlantic flight on a Navy NC-4. He was awarded the Navy Cross and the Congressional Medal of Achievement for "distinguished service in making the first successful trans-Atlantic flight." In addition to being a test pilot, he was a pioneer of modern air-sea rescue tactics. At Cape May in April 1933, Stone put his open-ocean landing skills to the test when the Navy dirigible *Akron* went down off the Atlantic coast in a storm. He was the only pilot available willing to attempt a landing in the heavy seas to rescue survivors.

This aerial photograph shows the base and air station as they appeared in 1936. It was during the height of the Great Depression, and lack of maintenance funds caused accelerated deterioration, particularly in many of the base's wooden buildings, which were constructed on top of dredged fill used to build up the marshlands when Section Base Nine was built in 1917. When Works Progress Administration (WPA) funds for labor became available, nearly every building had to be repaired from damage caused by termites, dry rot, or settlement. Buildings constructed on pile foundations were largely unaffected, however. Many of the original World War I–era buildings were sold and dismantled, while others were lost to fire. (Courtesy of the Library of Congress.)

Looking northwest in 1939, this aerial photograph, possibly taken from on top of the dirigible hangar, shows the many barracks surrounding the *T*-shaped mess hall and the two washhouses directly behind it. In front of the water tower is the YMCA building, where servicemen were offered a variety of activities. In the distance to the right is the Corinthian Yacht Club, which housed a boy's camp at that time.

An OJ-2 aircraft tows a sleeve used for fixed gunnery exercises in 1937 in front of the dirigible hangar. These targets were typically made of wire mesh, covered with cotton fabric, and weighted on the bottom by a heavy lead weight for stabilization. Each pilot's bullets were dipped in different colored printer's ink so their accuracy could be assessed afterwards.

An officer gives instructions to Coast Guardsmen inside the dirigible hangar in 1937. Behind him is a pair of Berliner-Joyce OJ-1 or OJ-2 lightweight observation biplanes. Put into service in the early 1930s, these were powered by a 400-horsepower Pratt and Whitney R-985 Wasp Jr. engine and had a fabric-covered fuselage with staggered wings.

The immense dirigible hangar, seen here in the late 1930s, also contained offices and ready rooms where flyers would be briefed about training exercises and rescue operations. The open windows suggest that the photograph was taken in the summer, and one pilot appears to have preferred a bicycle for transport around the base.

Seen here in front of Building 19—the dispensary—is an unidentified company of US Coast Guard air station servicemen, possibly graduates from an aviation school established in the 1930s there, and a variety of high-ranking officers. The building to the left is identified as the "receiving building" on the 1921 site plan, but it is not known if it still served as such in 1937.

A group of Marines in squadron VNS-3R march in the morning from the barracks to the hangar in 1937. Behind them are the large power plant and water tower. The Marines briefly occupied the base beginning in 1937, conducting their Officer's Training School there in the summer and using the target range for small arms practice.

Emerging from one of the seaplane hangars in March 1939 is this PH-2, which was purchased by the US Coast Guard from the Hall Aluminum Aircraft Corporation of Bristol, Pennsylvania. This type of amphibian aircraft was originally developed for the Navy as a patrol aircraft. Its initial acceptance trials took place at Air Station Cape May.

Named *Antares* after a star, this PJ-1, a large airplane for the day, became operational in June 1932. A seaplane, it was a high-wing monoplane with a gross weight of just over 11,000 pounds and a range of 1,000 nautical miles. Its engines were mounted in a pusher configuration. (Courtesy of the Mid-Atlantic Center for the Arts and Humanities.)

Seen here in the mid-1930s are four different types of Coast Guard aircraft parked inside the dirigible hangar. They are, from left to right, five Boeing F4B-3 or F4B-4 series; an NJ-1, the predecessor of the famous SNJ trainer series; two J2F Grumman "Ducks"; and either a Lockheed Model 10 or the R-30 twin-engine airplane.

The general utility J2K-2 aircraft seen here, made by the Fairchild Aircraft Corporation, was one of two purchased by the Coast Guard in 1936. The single-wing aircraft was used by the Navy for research and instrument training. It was also used for light transport by the Army. (Courtesy of the Wildwood Historical Society.)

Shown here in the dirigible hangar are two North American Aviation O-47Bs observation monoplanes with standard pre–World War II markings on the rudder. This variant carried more fuel and was powered by a larger engine than the O-47A. Both had all-metal construction with retractable landing gear. In World War II, they were used mainly as trainers and target tugs.

The massive doors sheltering the interior of the dirigible hangar were opened manually by six US Coast Guard men who pushed a turnstile. Seen here in 1937, they were capable of opening each door two feet per minute. Since the hangar was 133 feet wide, it took them about 30 minutes to open the doors all the way.

This late 1930s aerial photograph taken from high above the US Coast Guard base shows the air station after it was decommissioned in 1938 due to lack of funding. Note how close the air base runways were to the Atlantic Ocean (right). Erosion of the runways and the land near the firing range from hurricanes, nor'easters, and excessively high coastal tides was a constant problem.

Seen from the catwalk at the top of the dirigible hangar are two Grumman FF-1/SF-1 aircraft, Grumman's first aircraft designed for the Navy. Introduced in the early 1930s, they featured two seats with an enclosed cockpit, a fuselage of all-metal construction, and wings covered largely with fabric. They reached a top speed of almost 200 miles per hour, faster than any Navy fighter in service at the time.

The PH-2 above is being refueled on blocks at the ramp outside of the seaplane hangar at Cape May in 1939. This type of amphibian aircraft was originally developed for the Navy as a patrol aircraft. The upgraded flying boats purchased by the Coast Guard had more powerful engines as well as more specialized equipment and capabilities for search-and-rescue duties than the earlier Navy models, and were therefore given the designation PH-2. They were long-range aircraft capable of operating up to 1,000 miles from base and taking off and landing in rough seas. At the time, they were also the largest aircraft ever acquired by the Coast Guard.

A group of Navy Reserve men pose in front of a Hall PH-2 parked on the grass at Cape May in the mid-1930s. All are unidentified except for the man labeled "Dad," who is George Pedano (1902–1991), a Philadelphian who was a welder when he entered the Navy Reserve in 1934.

Enlisted as AMM3c .... Date 24 Sept. 1934
At Philadelphia, Penna. .... for four years
Born 17 October 1902 .... at Philadelphia, Penna.
Ratings held AMM 3c: AMM 2c: AMM 1c

Special duties for which qualified .... **************

Trade or Service Schools attended .... **************

Served on active or training duty on the following vessels and stations: (Inclusive dates)
                    VN-5RD4 - 8-17-35 to 8-30-35:
                    VN-5RD4 - 8-22-36 to 9-4-36:
                    VS-5R - 8-21-37 to 9-3-37:
                    VS-5R - 8-20-38 to 9-2-38.
Total number of drills and equivalent instruction or duty periods performed ... --
Final average in all marks upon discharge 3.6

DESCRIPTIVE LIST

Strike out one { ~~Made from examination~~~~or may or may not be~~ }
{ Made from record, if not present, at date of discharge.

Height 5 feet 6 inches. Weight 132 lbs.
Eyes Brown   Hair Black   Complexion Dark
Personal marks, etc. ....
Has / Has not } disqualifying defects (?)
(Not present for examination) .... (List here defects)
                              T. J. VAN METRE, Lieut. {U.S.N.
                              (Signature Medical Officer or Commanding Officer) {XXXXX

Monthly rate of pay when discharged $84.00
    I hereby certify that .... **************
has been paid .... dollars and .... cents ($. ....) in full to date.
                              OR
    I hereby certify that ----------- George Pedano -----------
was not in an active duty status at date of discharge.
                              (Strike out one)
23 Sept. - , 19 38 Total net services for pay purposes - years - months - days.
                              T. J. VAN METRE, Lt. {U.S.N.
                              (Supply or Commanding Officer's Signature) {XXXXX

Pedano enlisted in the Navy Reserves in September 1934 and served until September 1938. His discharge papers, seen here, show that he enlisted in Philadelphia, was paid $84 a month, and was not on active duty status when he was discharged.

George Pedano, an aviator with the Navy Reserve, is seen here next to his NY-2 aircraft, built by the Consolidated Aircraft Corporation, which primarily manufactured seaplanes and flying boats. The NY-2's wingspan was five feet longer than the first model, designated NY-1, in order to carry the extra weight of two machine guns. The engine was also enlarged to a 220-horsepower Wright J-5 (R-790) to accommodate the extra load. A large number of these biplane trainers were used by the Navy to give primary flight instruction and training in seaplane techniques and gunnery. The pupil and instructor sat in tandem open cockpits, as seen in this photograph. The Navy purchased 186 NY-2s and had 108 in active use in 1929, with 35 more assigned to reserves and 25 more with special armament for gunnery training. These biplanes served through 1939, many in reserve units.

Charles Thrun (1886–1935) joined the Coast Guard in 1908 and became its first enlisted aviator in 1917. In the fall of 1934, while assigned to Cape May, he began testing the new Grumman JF-2 "Duck" seaplane, which held great promise for various Coast Guard missions. The station's past commander, Elmer Stone, set a speed record of over 191 miles per hour in a Duck that December. On January 19, 1935, Thrun was practicing touch-and-goes in the icy waters off of Cape May in one of the new Ducks. He made three perfect landings, but when he started his fourth takeoff, the plane flipped over and sunk, trapping him in the cockpit. Machinist's mate Kermit Parker was thrown clear of the wreck but was unable to free Thrun despite several attempts. The station's crash boat arrived within five minutes and freed Thrun, but repeated efforts to revive him failed. Called "Daddy Thrun" by many, he became the Coast Guard's first aviator to be killed in a crash. He was buried with full honors in Arlington Cemetery. (Courtesy of Ken Freeze.)

Charles Thrun flew this Grumman JF-2 "Duck," assigned No. 162. The Duck was a state-of-the-art amphibian aircraft that had a single 775-horsepower engine and a range of over 750 miles, making it a capable plane well suited to the special needs of Coast Guard missions. After Thrun's crash, No. 162 was repaired, and in October 1936, it was renumbered V-136 and flew for many more years with the Coast Guard.

US Navy Reserve Scouting Squadron Five poses in front of the dirigible hangar on August 30, 1939. Congress created the Navy Reserve in 1915, and a year later, with the prospect of World War I looming, it was formally organized. In 1916, the first official Navy Reservists hunted enemy U-boats from the cockpits of biplanes.

An ambulance and a Douglas RD-2 Dolphin aircraft of the US Coast Guard stand side-by-side in December 1936 at the seaplane hangar ramp. The Dolphin was introduced in 1930 as the "Sinbad" and was a pure flying boat without wheels—it was intended as a luxurious flying yacht. Douglas improved the aircraft, making it amphibious and naming it the Dolphin. This model had an all-metal hull with room for eight passengers and two flight crewmen. It was used extensively in search-and-rescue missions and as a flying lifeboat. One of the Dolphins was completed for the Navy as the first presidential aircraft for Pres. Franklin D. Roosevelt, seating five, although it was reportedly never used by the president. No. V-111, seen here, was christened the *Adhara*; it crashed in March 1937. (Courtesy of the Library of Congress.)

Three

WORLD WAR II

US Naval Air Station Cape May was recommissioned in September 1940 and had two patrol squadrons and two blimps attached. This 1943 aerial photograph shows the addition of new barracks, bachelor officer's quarters, and a mess hall west of Fraser Avenue as the Navy mobilized to fight World War II. Additional wharves were also built, as were new, longer runways to accommodate bomber aircraft.

This close-up aerial photograph taken in 1943 shows several Vought OS2U Kingfisher aircraft, a station fire truck, and a new one-story operations building that featured a three-story air traffic control tower. The Quonset huts probably served as ready rooms for the naval aviators or as repair shops. Several of the air station's runways are seen at the top of the photograph.

Almost daily reports of boats sinking or being attacked just outside the Delaware Bay brought heightened security measures to Cape May. The security watch was doubled, officers began wearing revolvers, and patrols monitored the perimeter from dusk to dawn. Seen here about 1943 are the barracks buildings and a carport in the process of being camouflaged with paint.

A young woman is given a look at the rear cockpit of a PBY "Catalina" in this photograph from December 1946. The Catalina was used by the Navy and the Coast Guard during World War II. Capable of carrying an airborne lifeboat under one wing, a majority of these planes operated air and sea rescues until they were phased out of use in 1954.

Snow-covered ground did not cancel practice on the firing range. The air station had a skeet range and a small arms range on the ocean side of the station. Here, servicemen honed their abilities to not only protect the base in the event of an attack but to improve their marksmanship skills whether waterborne or airborne.

There was much debate about whether to save or tear down the dirigible hangar once the air station was recommissioned in 1940. An inspection revealed that the structural steel was good, but everything else was in poor to useless condition. The estimated cost for repairs—$50,000—would only check further deterioration, and the electrical equipment for door operations needed to be overhauled. Its wood sheathing was an almost inextinguishable fire hazard, it was too small for the airships operating at the time, and it should have been reoriented to a northwest-to-southeast axis that would be more advantageous with the prevailing southwest winds. Ultimately, the cost to correct so many deficiencies was prohibitive, and the hangar was demolished in July 1941.

An ambulance is parked in front of the air station's camouflaged firehouse around 1944. The firemen responded not only to airplane crashes on the airfield but also to fires in station buildings. This firehouse boasted a Ford pumper capable of producing 750 gallons at 120 pounds of pressure through 1,500 feet of two-inch hose. It also had a chemical hose and Foamite equipment.

Wheel Watch was a 16-page newsletter published weekly by the US Naval Air Station Cape May for personnel at the base. Some of the content was provided by the Camp Newspaper Service of the War Department. Articles included local history and news, rest and relaxation activities, duty changes, softball team scores and standings, and announcements.

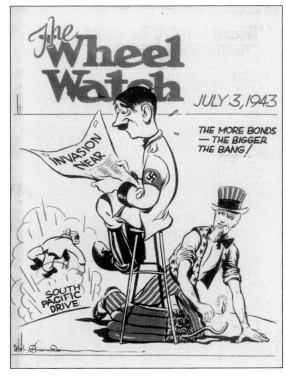

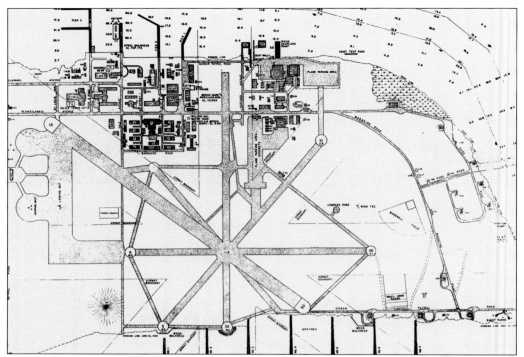

This site plan shows the naval air station during World War II. Concrete parking areas were installed for the planes, which could not park safely on the station's sandy soil. A large tract of land south of Yale (now Fraser) Avenue that included the former Corinthian Yacht Club was purchased during the war and became the site for many new buildings to accommodate the increase in manpower.

This aerial photograph, taken in the mid-1940s, shows the naval air station and its many buildings. Featured prominently in the foreground, to the right, is the dry dock. It was built to allow a vessel to be floated in, and then it was drained so the boat or craft could rest on a dry platform for maintenance and repair.

Two Vought F4U Corsairs, easily identified by their gull-shaped wings, are parked alongside a runway. The airplane's speed, firepower, maneuverability, and ruggedness cause many to rate it with the Mustang as the best fighter plane of World War II. As well as being an outstanding fighter capable of serving on a carrier, the Corsair proved to be an excellent fighter-bomber and was used almost exclusively in that role during the Korean War. It was the first Navy aircraft to feature landing gear that retracted into a fully enclosed wheelwell and the Navy had an 11-to-1 kill ratio with it. The Corsair featured an 18-cylinder double-radial engine capable of 2,250 horsepower with speeds of nearly 400 miles per hour—the largest engine available at the time. The first prototype was delivered to the Navy in 1940. Vought manufactured a total of 12,571 Corsairs in 16 separate models until 1953, making it the longest production run of any piston-engine fighter in US history.

At the canteen, servicemen could pause for a meal and a bit of friendly conversation, offering them a familiar and reassuring connection with home. Volunteers who served at the canteen enjoyed the opportunity to be of service to their country as they made a personal contribution to the war effort. This canteen was located in St. Ann's Roman Catholic Church in nearby Wildwood. (Courtesy of the Wildwood Historical Society.)

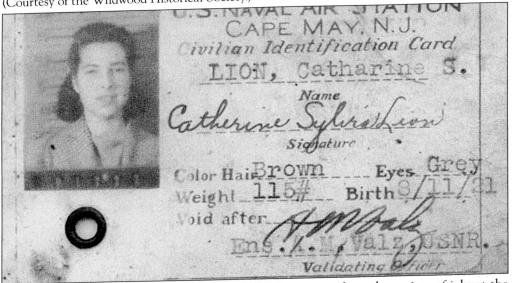

Civilians who carried an identification card like this one performed a variety of jobs at the Naval Air Station. Most lived nearby, either on one of the barrier islands or on the mainland, and performed clerical, secretarial, and janitorial tasks among other things. In mid-1944, the air station had 138 civilian personnel, 151 officers, and a complement of 349 aviation personnel out of a total of 1,050 enlisted.

An unidentified cutter steams past the air station during World War II, the black smoke from its stack advancing ahead under a stiff northwest wind. In January 1942, the afloat forces there consisted of an Eagle-class World War I vintage sub-chaser, three Coast Guard "75-footers," a 165-foot cutter, some minesweepers, and various Navy utility vessels. Soon after, the first 83-foot cutters began arriving. To accommodate larger ships and facilitate operations, the Cape May Harbor was dredged to 20 feet and the Cape May Canal was cut through with a depth of 12 feet under War Department contracts. The approaches to Delaware Bay were mined and a magnetic detector loop was laid to detect enemy submarines. For protection, all American ships were required to put into port at night beginning in February 1942. A great deal of effort was spent in sweeping the shipping channels because German submarines had laid mines at the mouth of the Delaware River, one of which struck a large tug in 1942.

Collectively, three generations of the Howell family from Cape May County have served in the Coast Guard, for a total of 253 years. Elroy Howell, the first to serve, is seen here in the center between his sons, from left to right, Buck, Howard, Bert, and Norman. Elroy served for 32 years and retired as a boson mate first class. Norman enlisted in 1930 and served with the rank of surfman at local lifesaving stations. He also served with the mounted beach patrol during World War II and told the story of finding clothing on the beach belonging to German U-boat sailors who came ashore one night to visit the local bars. He retired in 1957 as chief petty officer from the Cape May Coast Guard. Norman's four brothers—Howard, Leroy, Buck, and Bert—all served between 20 and 30 years in the Coast Guard. Norman's son, Dave Howell, continued the family tradition when he enlisted in 1960 and retired 20 years later as chief petty officer.

```
C H R I S T M A S   1 9 4 2

U.S. NAVAL AIR STATION, CAPE MAY, N.J.
                DINNER MENU


              FRESH FRUIT COCKTAIL
              CREAM OF TOMATO SOUP
                   SALTINES
CRISP ROLLS                           BUTTER
     HEARTS OF CELERY, RIPE OLIVES, SWEET PICKLES
          ROAST YOUNG PARAMOUNT TURKEY
                OYSTER FILLING
CRANBERRY JELLY                    GIBLET SAUCE
CANDIED CAROLINA YAMS              BUTTERED GREEN PEAS
HEARTS OF LETTUCE                  RUSSIAN DRESSING
OLD FASHION FRUIT CAKE             PUMPKIN PIE
ASSORTED HARD CANDIES              MIXED NUTS
                  ICE CREAM
                   COFFEE
CIGARS                             CIGARETTES
```

Christmas spent away from home was hard on station morale, so everything was done to make the holiday as comforting as possible. The menu from the station's 1942 Christmas dinner shows that Navy men were treated to a five-course meal that included fruit cocktail, cream of tomato soup, roast young turkey with oyster filling, yams, peas, cranberry jelly, and lettuce with Russian dressing. Three kinds of dessert were offered: fruitcake, pumpkin pie, and ice cream. Cigars and cigarettes were also made available. The oyster dressing was particularly appropriate because a large amount of oysters were harvested every year in the nearby Delaware Bay.

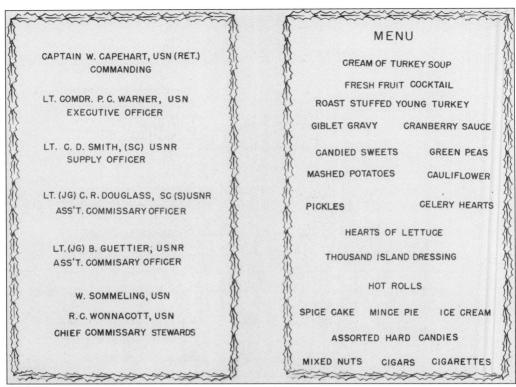

CAPTAIN W. CAPEHART, USN (RET.)
COMMANDING

LT. COMDR. P. C. WARNER, USN
EXECUTIVE OFFICER

LT. C. D. SMITH, (SC) USNR
SUPPLY OFFICER

LT. (JG) C. R. DOUGLASS, SC (S) USNR
ASS'T. COMMISSARY OFFICER

LT. (JG) B. GUETTIER, USNR
ASS'T. COMMISARY OFFICER

W. SOMMELING, USN

R. C. WONNACOTT, USN

CHIEF COMMISSARY STEWARDS

MENU

CREAM OF TURKEY SOUP

FRESH FRUIT COCKTAIL

ROAST STUFFED YOUNG TURKEY

GIBLET GRAVY   CRANBERRY SAUCE

CANDIED SWEETS   GREEN PEAS

MASHED POTATOES   CAULIFLOWER

PICKLES   CELERY HEARTS

HEARTS OF LETTUCE

THOUSAND ISLAND DRESSING

HOT ROLLS

SPICE CAKE   MINCE PIE   ICE CREAM

ASSORTED HARD CANDIES

MIXED NUTS   CIGARS   CIGARETTES

The Christmas dinner served in the general mess hall in 1944 was not much different from that served in 1942. The main course still included roast stuffed turkey with sweet potatoes, peas, giblet gravy, and cranberry sauce. Thousand Island dressing was substituted for Russian dressing over the salad. Spice cake, mincemeat pie, and ice cream, along with assorted hard candies and mixed nuts, finished the meal. The menu's back cover featured the station's mascot, a pirate wearing aviator goggles dropping a bomb. Listed inside were the station's officers, headed by Capt. Wadleigh Capehart (1888–1952), one of the Navy's first 20 aviators, who was called back from retirement when war broke out.

CHRISTMAS 1944

GENERAL MESS

NAVAL AIR STATION
CAPE MAY, NEW JERSEY

During World War II, select Coast Guard men, mostly experienced riders, were trained for the mounted beach patrol. Riding on horseback, these men would patrol the shoreline to supplement other land, sea, and air patrols already in operation. Checkpoints were located strategically on the beaches and the crisscrossing of patrols made any activity virtually impossible to go unnoticed. They were constantly on the alert for any raft landings or signals either from sea or land. Patrols operated mostly at night under all weather conditions, with the horses withstanding the elements better than their riders in inclement weather. During the day, the riders were drilled on horseback and instructed in the care, feeding, and stabling of their mounts. Their uniforms were dress blue jackets, riding breeches, trousers, leather boots, and visor hats, duplicated in khaki for summer wear. The shoreline from Rehoboth Beach in Delaware north to Brigantine in Atlantic County, New Jersey, was patrolled until the operation was discontinued in the spring of 1944.

The December 1944 issue of *Wheel Watch*, the air station's newsletter, included this advertisement on the back cover. War loan drives were conducted throughout World War II as a way of raising money to pay for the war effort. Pres. Franklin D. Roosevelt announced the sixth war loan drive on November 19, 1944, and hoped to sell $14 billion in war bonds.

The cover of this *Wheel Watch* newsletter plays on the US Navy's claim in September 1943 that it had become the greatest sea-air power on earth. That year, the Navy had more than 13 times as many ships as it had two years earlier and boasted an air force of 18,269 planes, along with a fleet of 14,072 vessels that included 613 fighting ships.

This cartoon, from inside the June 2, 1945, *Wheel Watch*, reflected the decrease in the number of men, or complement, at the station beginning in early 1945. As ever-increasing numbers of enlisted men were needed for sea duty and new ship construction, personnel at the station were reduced accordingly.

Two Curtiss SB2C Helldivers taxi on the air station's runway in 1945. The Helldiver had a reputation for being difficult to handle at low speeds but was responsible for destroying more Japanese targets than any other aircraft during World War II. It carried two men and had a top speed of 295 miles per hour.

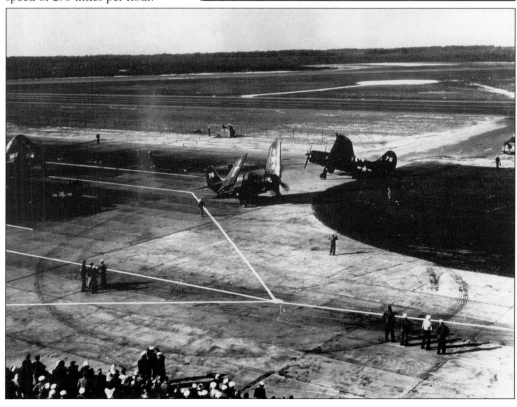

Members of the US Coast Guard Auxiliary pose in one of the Cape May Air Station buildings in the mid-1940s. The auxiliary is the uniformed volunteer branch of the Coast Guard, established as the Coast Guard Reserve by Congress in 1939. The legislation gave the Coast Guard a mandate to use civilians to promote safety on and over the high seas and the nation's navigable waters. Congress also authorized the auxiliary to support all Coast Guard missions not related to direct engagement in either law enforcement activities or military combat operations. Two years later, the reserve was redesignated as the auxiliary. During World War II, 50,000 people joined the auxiliary, and many of their private vessels were placed into service in an effort to protect the United States from enemy vessels. (Courtesy of the Wildwood Historical Society.)

Four

THE US COAST GUARD RETURNS

In 1945, when this aerial photograph of the air station was taken, planning began to phase down after victory in Europe was declared on May 8. The naval air stations at Cape May and at nearby Wildwood were removed from the list of "stations deemed wise to retain permanently," and in September 1945, both were designated as surplus. By June 1946, all remaining personnel left the base.

On December 14, 1945, the *Cape May County Gazette* announced that the Coast Guard would again take over the base, as it had before the war. The base was to be used as "a headquarters for surface craft, air craft, the buoy service and other Coast Guard activities designed to promote the safety of boatmen and seafarers in the Cape May sector." On June 1, 1946, the base was officially turned over to the Coast Guard under the leadership of Comdr. Joseph McCue, a Coast Guard aviator who had been stationed at Cape May in 1937 and 1938. In 1946, the station had an air-sea rescue detachment and several 111-foot crash boats. This photograph, taken in the late 1940s, shows the commanding officer's house in the center with a chicken coop and dog pens next to the garage. Several patrol boats are tied to the dock, awaiting an assignment.

In 1947, visitors to the Coast Guard base had to check in at the gatehouse, at the main entrance on Pennsylvania Avenue (now Munro Drive). This view looks west down Pennsylvania Avenue toward Cape May. The street is lined with telephone poles, and the brush-covered vacant building lots show how desolate the area immediately outside the base was.

The magazine and its lookout booth, seen here in 1949, was one of several built during World War II that stood on the perimeter of the base overlooking the Cape May Canal and the Atlantic Ocean. The earth berm provided protection and containment should any of the ordnance stored inside explode.

This two-story dormitory, seen here in the summer of 1948, was built to accommodate the increase in manpower at the air station during World War II. The World War I–era, one-story building in front of it still bears the camouflage paint applied as a security measure in 1943. Because of a lack of steel for construction, many buildings like this one were made of concrete or terra-cotta block during the war.

The mess hall, seen here in 1948, was built during World War I after the original Section Base Nine buildings burned in a fire on July 4, 1918. The mess hall was larger than it appears in this photograph and had a rear ell. The building faced north onto Pennsylvania Avenue (now Munro Drive); today, its site is a vacant lot just east of Munro Hall.

This large concrete-block hangar, just east of the site of the dirigible hangar, was built during the period of modernization and expansion of the base prior to World War II. The one-story shed-roofed section around the perimeter is original to the building and probably provided peripheral support for the hangar. The ladder structure on the roof was likely used for observation. This photograph was taken in 1949.

In May 1949, all that remained of the former Corinthian Yacht Club were the brick basement walls, seen here with their arched openings. The land on which the club stood was purchased by the federal government during World War II to expand the air station. It is not known why the upper stories were demolished or what purpose the basement served when this photograph was taken.

Piles of trash, including office chairs, bureaus, and desks, suggest that this remote area south of the runways was used as a dump after the Navy vacated the air station in 1946. Seen in the distance in this 1949 photograph are the firing range and two bunkers overlooking the Atlantic Ocean.

The purpose of this small brick building, seen here in 1949, is not known. The double doors bear a sign that says "Danger," so it may have held electrical equipment of some sort. The ruins of another small building and its poured concrete floor are all that can be seen across the street. The speed along the road is marked at 20 miles per hour.

In 1949, several buildings from the World War I era remained on the site. One of the largest was the arch-roofed seaplane hangar. Built of wood frame construction, it overlooked the harbor and had a wooden ramp for launching seaplanes into the water for training exercises and search-and-rescue missions.

Another view of the seaplane hangar, this one in 1949, shows the east side of the building. In front of it is all that remains of another seaplane hangar built at the same time that appears to have been sold for scrap after World War II. The row of three connected buildings in the center is a boathouse built in 1945 and used to store smaller craft.

Seen here in 1949 are concrete pilings and a concrete pad—all that remains of two air station buildings that were sold for scrap after World War II. The one-story wooden building in the foreground was built in 1918 and is labeled on the 1921 site plan as being used for oil storage, a use confirmed by the loading dock and double entrance visible on the east side of the building.

This unidentified building was erected in 1942 or 1943 on the site of the original public works building and had approximately the same footprint. At the time, the base was expanding rapidly, with its complement of men expected to rise from 150 to 1,000. New buildings erected at the time included a dispensary, a recreation hall, a supply building, a school building, a hangar, and an inert storehouse.

Vacant in the late 1930s, this two-story wooden building was erected during World War I and stood behind Seaplane Hangar No. 1. On the 1921 site plan, it is identified as Building No. 130 and was being used as the paint and carpenter shop. Its use during World War II is not known and it was reportedly used for target practice once it was abandoned after the war.

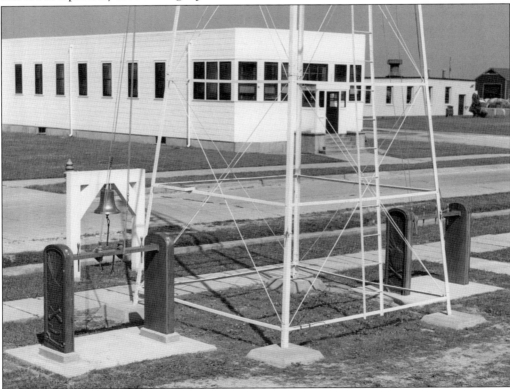

The ship's bell was rung every hour. Seen here in May 1949, it stands in front of the metal tower that serves as the flagpole. Note the metal stanchions on each side—they appear to date to the World War I era and have special fasteners onto which the flag ropes were secured. The building in the background housed the infirmary, administrative offices, and a communications office.

During World War I, these two-story barracks were built four-deep and flanked each side of the mess hall. They faced north onto Pennsylvania Avenue (now Munro Drive) and featured elements commonly found in the Neoclassical style, popular in residences and public buildings from 1895 to about 1950. Details that characterize the style include exterior-wall brick chimneys, two-story porches often accessed by French doors, hipped roofs, and multipaned windows placed in pairs. Earlier photographs show that the porches were originally a full two stories tall, with taller columns extending up to a roof that covered the porch. The columns were probably shortened during World War II. The revival of interest in classical styles dates to the 1893 World's Fair, which featured dramatic, colonnaded buildings placed around a central court, inspiring countless public and commercial buildings in the following decades. This photograph was taken in 1949, shortly after the Coast Guard returned to the base.

Coast Guardsmen gather in 1949 in front of what was the oldest boathouse still standing on the base at the time. It was built during World War I and, with the new boathouse behind it, served throughout World War II. Boathouses like this one were used to store small craft out of the elements.

This photograph, taken in May 1949, shows the former Coast Guard lifesaving station in Cape May, known then as the Cold Spring station. On Beach Avenue between Madison and Philadelphia Avenues, it is a Bibb No. 2–style station, named after designer Albert Bibb. There were nine Bibb stations built along the Jersey shore between 1886 and 1891. This one still stands and is now used by the Kiwanis Club.

In the early days, telephone traffic was carried over copper conducting wire, which shows resistance to electrical signals. Since the power of transmitted signals diminishes the farther it travels, the telephone repeater station, seen here in 1949, was used to amplify, or repeat, voice signals to bring them up to their original strength.

The base was heated by coal-fired, steam-generating boilers like the one seen here in 1949 in Boiler House No. 1. The boiler probably dates to World War I. Coal was brought in by boat and unloaded into a storage area adjacent to the boiler house. The man tending the boiler is seen here checking the burning coal inside.

This supply building, seen here in 1948, was built in 1942–1943, when plans to expand the station were the most ambitious. At the time, new construction and additional facilities recommended were estimated to cost well over $4 million and included at least a dozen new buildings, the extension of two runways, and the addition of groins along the Atlantic shoreline to prevent erosion of the beachfront.

At the far left in this December 1948 photograph is the motion picture theater, which was built to help entertain the more than 1,000 men stationed here during World War II. It was conveniently located close to the barracks. The barracks seen here were built during World War I and several are still covered in the camouflage paint added for security during World War II.

Another view of the gatehouse, seen here in the late 1940s, shows the Coast Guard base buildings in the distance. A variety of patrol boats are seen to the far left tied up at the dock. The commanding officer's quarters, partially hidden by the telephone pole, overlook the lot where the former Corinthian Yacht Club's clubhouse used to stand.

In 1948, the Coast Guard recruit-training base at the naval air station in Mayport, Florida, was closed and relocated to Cape May. This photograph, taken that year, shows the nine-member basketball team from the Cape May recruit center. Sports teams were an integral part of after-hours activities at all military bases, offering much-needed recreation and competition for servicemen.

A Coast Guardsman keeps tally while others practice their marksmanship skills on the rifle range in the early 1950s. Seen in the distance to the far right is the six-story Christian Admiral Hotel in Cape May. It was leased by the Navy for bachelor officers' quarters in 1942; soon after, pilots with their families as well as officers from the nearby naval air station in Wildwood were also quartered there.

The rifle range is seen here in May 1950, with 10 targets placed atop a tall earth berm, each identified by a number for scoring purposes. The earth berm overlooked the Atlantic Ocean, and the waters in the vicinity of the range were closed to boats while the range was being used.

The watchtower, seen here around 1950, was three stories tall and offered a 360-degree view of the base and airfield. Coast Guard trainees had to learn how to operate the watchtower before they graduated; they were also trained in how to send signals from it. The Quonset hut was used for storage while the purpose of the building behind the tower is not known.

A group of Coast Guardsmen, likely recruits, stand in formation outside of the large hangar that was built at the east end of the air station during World War II. The training center had facilities for 500 personnel and was capable of handling up to 200 recruits monthly; recruits trained for five to six weeks.

The newly reestablished Coast Guard base is seen here in 1947. All buildings that had been painted in camouflage colors during World War II were repainted in white. The large light-colored cutter seen to the right is the USS *Mohawk*, a 165-foot "A"-class cutter built by the Pusey and Jones Corporation in Wilmington, Delaware, in 1934. It was commissioned in 1935 and decommissioned in January 1948. Its first assignment was patrolling and general icebreaking on the Hudson and Delaware Rivers and it was stationed at Cape May when World War II began. It was then assigned to North Atlantic Escort operations with the Greenland patrol and served there for the entire war, launching a total of 14 submarine attacks between August 1942 and April 1945. Reassignment to Cape May came in the winter of 1945, and in April 1946, the *Mohawk* was placed "in reserve, in commission" status with a skeleton crew at Cape May. It will be sunk to create an artificial reef in 2012. (Courtesy of the Mid-Atlantic Center for the Arts and Humanities.)

In March 1951, the training center had four busy piers. The *F*-shaped pier in the foreground is Pier Four, the largest, which was built in the early 1940s as part of the air station expansion. Immediately behind it is Pier Three, built at the same time. The other two piers were erected in 1918.

At least two kinds of buoys are stacked like dominoes in front of the aids-to-navigation building seen here in the 1950s. The nun, can, and spar buoys are the oldest style of minor navigation aids in America's coastal waters. Durable but unlit, these buoys are probably among the most familiar to the non-mariner. (Courtesy of the US Coast Guard.)

This aerial photograph shows the Coast Guard base as it appeared in the early-to-mid-1950s. The cutter identified as W401 is the USCG *Sassafras*, a C-class, 180-foot seagoing buoy tender constructed in 1943 for the Coast Guard by the Marine Iron and Shipbuilding Corporation of Duluth, Minnesota. It was one of 39 tenders commissioned for duties that included aids-to-navigation, ice-breaking, search-and-rescue, firefighting, and law enforcement. Cape May became its homeport in 1947. Among other things, it assisted the cutter *Eastwind* in 1949 after it was severely damaged in a collision, and in 1957, it assisted two Air Force aircraft in the Delaware Bay after a midair collision. In 1977, it left Cape May for a major renovation that included the complete removal and overhaul of all mechanical systems, including the main engines. It was decommissioned in 2003 after 59 years of service and is now the Navy ship *Obula* in the Federal Republic of Nigeria.

The more than 80 members of Company F-31 are seen here at their May 1, 1957, graduation from the US Coast Guard Training Center. They are seated on bleachers that overlook one of the abandoned World War II runways. Behind them are the infirmary and administration building.

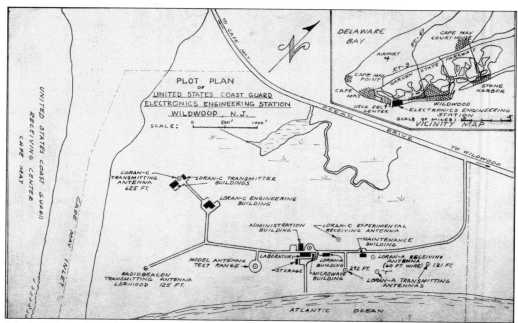

The US Coast Guard Electronics Engineering Center was established as a test station in Virginia in 1943 and was moved to a 392-acre site across from the Cape May Coast Guard Station in 1948. Its mission was to provide engineering logistic support through the development of new electronic systems and devices, particularly for electronic aids to marine navigation like LORAN and marine radar systems. The center was disestablished in 1997.

Designed in 1947 by sculptor Norman M. Thomas, this bronze statue in front of the gymnasium is dedicated "in memory of Coast Guardsmen who served in World War II." It is a smaller, almost-identical version of a larger statue—also a US Coast Guard memorial—in New York City's Battery Park. Thomas served in the Coast Guard during World War II. The monument depicts an interracial three-figure group in which two soldiers wearing fatigues and bearing rifles support a wounded soldier. Thomas, a nonprofessional sculptor, was a painter and combat veteran who studied at the American Academy in Rome and with Paul Manship at the National Academy of Design in New York City. He based his composition on a rescue he had witnessed at the Luzon beachhead. Relying on a sketch that Thomas submitted, the Coast Guard commissioned the sculpture. The Coast Guard maintains an administrative facility just south of Battery Park, and until the late 1990s, had a base on Governors Island in New York Harbor.

The recruit training center gym was originally in the former hangar at the east end of the complex, which was built during World War II. Seen here in February 1953, it featured bleachers, a boxing ring, a punching bag, and a basketball court, all of which were used by recruits during training and after hours.

Housing for servicemen and their families was a large problem during World War II at the air station, and about a dozen small, single-family homes like these were built on Delaware Avenue near the intersection of Pittsburgh Avenue west of the station. The water tower at the training center is in the distance. (Courtesy of the US Coast Guard Training Center.)

The first lifesaving mission with a Coast Guard helicopter was performed by aviator Frank Erickson in 1944. Seen here is the HO4S-3 Sikorsky helicopter powered by a 700-horsepower Wright R-1300 engine. They were designed for observation and search-and-rescue missions and could easily operate from small areas like the deck of a cutter. They had a cruising speed of 80 knots with a top speed of 115 knots, and a more-than-400-mile flying range. Equipped for instrument and night flying, they included such equipment as a hydraulic hoist to pick up personnel or equipment weighing up to 400 pounds. They were painted bright yellow and were the largest helicopters operating in the Coast Guard at the time. Later refinements to the helicopter saw the addition of slings and rescue baskets. They were also used to test the practicality of towing vessels and could tow a vessel of up to 800 tons a distance of up to 20 miles.

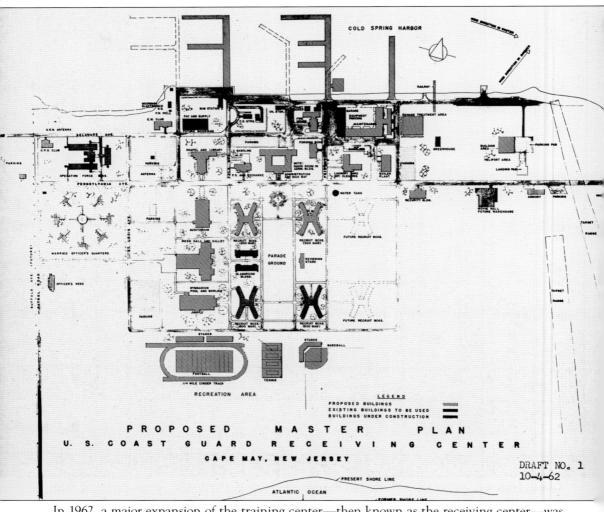

PROPOSED MASTER PLAN
U. S. COAST GUARD RECEIVING CENTER
CAPE MAY, NEW JERSEY

DRAFT NO. 1
10-4-62

In 1962, a major expansion of the training center—then known as the receiving center—was proposed. According to this proposed master plan, more than 20 new buildings were planned, including two new recruit barracks capable of holding 500 men each, an auditorium, a mess hall and galley, a gymnasium with a pool and a bowling alley, married officers' quarters, a post office and exchange, an administration and sick bay, laundry and dry cleaning facilities, a boiler plant, a security building, an officers' mess, chief petty officers' club, enlisted men's club, a firehouse, and an armory. According to the site plan, two of the X-shaped dormitories, two classroom buildings, a movie hall, and the operating force/permanent party barracks were already under construction and the location of two future recruit barracks had been identified. Also proposed were a football field, tennis courts, and a baseball field at the south side of the complex. The existing three docks were slated to be eliminated and rebuilt along the harbor. Many of the proposed buildings were never erected.

Munro Hall was one of three X-shaped dormitories built in the 1960s, accommodating 500 recruits on three floors. The hall is named for Douglas A. Munro (1919–1942), a signalman first class in the Coast Guard who died heroically on Guadalcanal on September 27, 1942, when he volunteered to rescue a detachment of US Marines. While under heavy enemy fire, he brought boats on shore and proceeded to evacuate the men from the beach. Most of them were in the boats when complications arose while evacuating the last men, whom Munro quickly realized would be in the greatest danger. He accordingly placed himself and his boats so they would serve as cover for the last men to leave. In doing so, he was fatally wounded, and the men were safely evacuated. He remained conscious only long only to say four words: "Did they get off?" He died without knowing that his mission had succeeded and his final assignment had been carried out. (Courtesy of the US Coast Guard Training Center.)

Taken in the late 1960s, this aerial photograph shows the new buildings that were erected earlier in the decade. The three distinctive X-shaped dormitories, taller than everything but the water tower in this scene, dominate the landscape. The former World War II runways are barely discernible, having been built upon or grassed in the more than 20 years since they were used.

This 1964 aerial photograph prominently features the *Unimak* (No. 379) and the darker-colored boat known as the unibarge. When the center's machine shop burned in 1961, the unibarge was brought in. It was a floating machine shop and repair facility for all of the boats. The new administration building is the large darker building to the left.

USCG W-379, known as the *Unimak*, is seen in this postcard. Built as a small seaplane tender for the Navy in 1942 and commissioned in 1943, it was then commissioned into the Coast Guard on January 3, 1949. It was home-ported in Boston from 1949 until 1956, where it was used for law enforcement and search-and-rescue operations. From 1956 until 1972, the *Unimak* was stationed at Cape May, where it was used primarily for training reservists, taking training cruises to Brazil and Nova Scotia. In 1967, the *Unimak* rescued six Cuban refugees in the Yucatan Channel, rescued survivors from a ship in Florida waters, and then rescued 12 Cuban refugees stranded on an island. From 1972 until 1975, it was stationed at Yorktown, Virginia, again training reservists. In the 1980s, the *Unimak* was responsible for seizing more than 1,000 bales and over 42 tons of marijuana in seven separate incidents in the Caribbean. It was returned to the Navy in April 1988 and was later expended as an artificial reef off the Virginia coast.

The original chapel, seen in this mid-1950s postcard, was built in 1918 as the YMCA for Section Base Nine. It stood on Pennsylvania Avenue (now Munro Drive) and was later used as an enlisted men's club and theater. In 1948, it was converted into the training center's chapel and was used in that capacity until the new chapel was built in 1982.

Likely taken in the 1960s, this photograph shows the 34-member recruit band as it marches south down Yale (now Fraser) Avenue. Behind them is the firehouse, built in 1918, which still stands, although greatly altered from its original appearance. To the band's left is the brig and post office, now the site of Munro Hall.

This postcard, printed in the 1960s, shows four different types of Coast Guard boats from that time period. To the far right is an aids-to-navigation boat that would have been used to maintain buoys and day markers in the inland waterways. Next to it, to the left, is a 44-foot self-righting surfboat that is able to roll in heavy surf and end up right-side-up. It has been replaced by a 48-foot self-righting surfboat. The next two boats are small vessels used for patrol and search-and-rescue. The first one appears to be a 21-footer that was used almost universally. Behind them is the permanent party barracks, built in the early 1960s, and to the far right, the new Corinthian Yacht Club, which was built to replace the original structure purchased by the Coast Guard during World War II.

The HH52-A Seagard, made by Sikorsky Aircraft Corporation of Stratford, Connecticut, was used by the Coast Guard primarily for air-sea rescues. It was the backbone of the Coast Guard's rotary-winged fleet from the time of its introduction in 1963 until the final helicopter was retired in 1989. In all, 99 of these versatile helicopters saw service. The aircraft was first conceived and designed to be amphibious so that flotation gear would not be required for overwater flights, allowing rescues to be made by landing on the water. The fuselage is watertight for landings on water or snow and two outrigger floats resist pitching and rolling on the water. It held a crew of three and had a range of 474 miles.

The machine shop, seen at right around 1960, was built during World War II as a moorings, boat, and equipment building and stood at the foot of Pier Three. After being converted to an engine repair shop, it caught fire in March 1961 and, despite efforts from land and water, was totally consumed by fire. Machinist's mate first class Lawrence Franklin and fireman apprentice Harvey Johnson were on call in case of mechanical trouble at the center and were sleeping in the building when the fire started. Unfortunately, both Coast Guardsmen lost their lives in the blaze. No one else was in the building at the time.

Named for eminent geologist and educator Jean Louis Agassiz (1807–1873), the *Agassiz* was built by the American Brown Boveri Electric Corporation in Camden, New Jersey, in 1926 and commissioned in January 1927. A 125-foot-long patrol boat, its class of vessels was one of the most useful and long-lasting in Coast Guard service, with 16 cutters still in use in the 1960s. Constructed at a cost of $63,173, it was designed for trailing the "mother ship" along the outer line of patrol during Prohibition. All but two of the 33 built served in World War II. The *Agassiz's* first homeport was Boston, but it was transferred to Cape May in October 1956 and was based there until it was decommissioned in October 1969. While in Cape May, it assisted the yawl *Septic Nerve*, which had grounded in Little Egg Inlet, New Jersey, in 1961. In 1967, the *Agassiz* assisted the disabled Canadian fishing vessel *Clara and Linda* about 160 miles east of New York during a storm.

CG-44318, seen here off the South Jersey coast around 1970, was one of 110 motor lifeboats, all 44 feet long, built between 1963 and 1972 and used at Coast Guard stations throughout the United States for nearly 40 years. It is one of the most legendary boats ever introduced into American coastal rescue service. A unique craft in the overall development of American coastal lifeboats, it was used successfully around the nation and had a worldwide influence on the design of search-and-rescue craft. The development of the 44-footer is a prime example of a vessel being designed for very specific conditions. Self-righting and self-bailing, it could operate successfully in coastal waters under unusually severe weather and sea conditions. It was designed to operate in light ice or heavy surf and could survive accidental groundings. Very few 44-foot motor lifeboats were lost or severely damaged enough to prevent restoration to service, and the last of this class—CG-44301—was decommissioned in spring 2010. (Courtesy of the Mid-Atlantic Center for the Arts and Humanities.)

This postcard from the mid-1960s shows recruits lined up around the World War II–era boathouse. The two boats tied to the dock are 30-footers, one made of fiberglass and the other of steel. The boat in the foreground is a 26-foot motor launch that appears to have been a "captain's gig"—a wooden cruiser found on 327-foot cutters that was reserved for the captain as his launch.

The Coast Guard band and honor guard are seen here in the late 1960s or early 1970s marching down Beach Avenue in Cape May. The Coast Guard Training Center at Cape May has no regular band but has always had a recruit band like this one, which was very popular at this time. The honor guard was composed of recruits as well.

Construction began in May 1967 on a new helicopter hangar that would also house maintenance shops, supply rooms, and air-conditioned offices for the seven officers and 30 enlisted men who staffed it. At the time, helicopters—some coming from as far away as Brooklyn, New York, at a travel time of 45 minutes—used a small pad at the training center. In emergencies, the flight time from other areas was deemed too long. With its own helicopter base, the training center was able to speed up rescue operations and greatly expand along the Atlantic coast. The project also included two new rescue helicopters that were purchased for $575,000 each. The new hangar was expected to cost approximately $700,000 and was going to take about 15 months to complete. The hangar project was part of an $8-million expansion program that was projected to take three years to accomplish.

A new dining room for Coast Guard recruits and permanent party was built in the mid-1970s. In 2012, it underwent a $65,000 renovation to the staff dining area and was rededicated to Richard Etheridge (1842–1900), a Union army veteran who became the first African American keeper of a lifesaving station. Born a slave, Etheridge served at the Pea Island Life Saving Station on the Outer Banks of North Carolina in the late 1800s. He developed rigorous drills that enabled his all–African American crew to master lifesaving skills. His station earned the reputation of "one of the tautest on the Carolina Coast," with its keeper well known as one of the most courageous and ingenious lifesavers in the service. In October 1896, Etheridge and his crew battled strong tides and sweeping currents 10 times to rescue the entire crew of the *E.S. Newman*, a three-masted schooner that beached during a fierce storm. For this rescue, Etheridge and his crew posthumously received the Coast Guard's Gold Lifesaving Medal in 1996. (Courtesy of the US Coast Guard Training Center.)

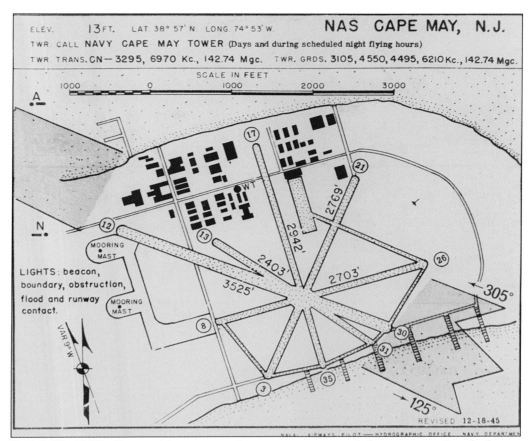

ELEV. 13 FT. LAT. 38° 57' N. LONG. 74° 53' W.

NAS CAPE MAY, N.J.

TWR. CALL NAVY CAPE MAY TOWER (Days and during scheduled night flying hours)

TWR. TRANS. CN — 3295, 6970 Kc., 142.74 Mgc. TWR. GRDS. 3105, 4550, 4495, 6210 Kc., 142.74 Mgc.

SCALE IN FEET

LIGHTS: beacon, boundary, obstruction, flood and runway contact.

REVISED 12-18-45

NAVAL AIRWAYS PILOT — HYDROGRAPHIC OFFICE NAVY DEPARTMENT

During World War II, two of the air station's runways were expanded to accommodate the longer takeoff and landing requirements of the Navy's powerful fighter jets that were stationed here. The map above, drawn in December 1945, shows the new, longer configurations of the runways, with extensions to the runways that ran north to south (17 to 35) and northwest to southeast (12 to 30). Taken in October 1964, the aerial view below shows what was originally the northwest end of the northwest-to-southeast runway (12). By this time, new dormitories had been built over parts of the runway. Bleachers along the sideline suggest that spectators gathered here for special events. The closer end with a circle and X was used for helicopter landings.

111

The USCG *Hornbeam* was built in 1943 at a cost of more than $864,000 by the Marine and Iron Shipbuilding Corporation in Duluth, Minnesota. It was commissioned by the Coast Guard in April 1944, and in 1945, it had a complement of six officers and 74 enlisted men. The 180-foot buoy tender was also capable of conducting search-and-rescue and law enforcement missions in addition to its primary mission of tending aids-to-navigation. This class was built of welded steel and could steam 8,000 miles at 13 knots. All served during World War II, many in the Atlantic theater, where they served as armed escorts for merchant convoys, hunted U-boats, and carried supplies to far-flung installations. Several vessels in the class were dispatched thousands of miles out into the Atlantic to collect important meteorological data that allowed military planners to schedule and route aircraft flights to Europe. The *Hornbeam* was stationed at Cape May from April 1977 until it was decommissioned in September 1999.

The US Coast Guard Training Center is seen here in this aerial photograph, looking east in 1967. The newly expanded base features several new dormitories and a new administration building, among others. At the time, the center had 1,100 recruits, 100 permanent staff, and 11 ships. The number of recruits was expected to double in the next five years because of the Vietnam War.

By the late 1960s, the southeast end of one of the extended runways was greatly eroded by the ever-encroaching Atlantic Ocean. This view shows the disintegration of the circular concrete runway end where planes would turn around before takeoff. Part of the rifle range is seen to the extreme right along the oceanfront.

Although women served in the Women's Reserve of the US Coast Guard during World War II, they were not officially integrated into active duty until 1973. That year, the first women since 1945 were admitted to Officer Candidate School and the first female enlistees were sworn into the regular Coast Guard. In 1974, the first group of women ever enlisted as "regulars" reported to Cape May on January 15, 1974, and mixed-gender basic training began. In April 1974, the first woman was assigned to a patrol boat, and in 1977, the first woman was designated as a Coast Guard aviator. In August 1978, the commandant announced that "all personnel restrictions based solely on sex would be lifted." Thereafter, all officer career fields and enlisted ratings were open to women. The aviator seen here in the late 1970s stands in front of her amphibious HH-52a helicopter, one of the Coast Guard's workhorses for air-sea rescue operations.

Beginning in the late 1970s and early 1980s, new family housing was erected in four phases on land sited west of the training center. Located on both sides of Delaware and Pennsylvania Avenues, the multiunit buildings consisted of several different models of attached, two-story frame houses. Phase I provided three- and four-bedroom dwellings used for junior officer and enlisted quarters; phases II and III provided three- and four-bedroom family housing; phase IV provided two-bedroom housing. All models except for the two-bedroom version featured a full bath on each floor and had a combined living and dining room. Concrete patios, often with exterior storage, were accessed by sliding glass doors off the rear of each unit. Each also had either a separate laundry room or laundry facilities in the kitchen. Photographs of the phase II and III buildings show them with solar electric panels, which have since been removed.

The members of the center's Facilities Engineering Department, which received the Cowart Award, are seen here in 1982. The award, first given in 1968, is presented annually by the Society of American Military Engineers in recognition of an outstanding contribution to the Coast Guard's civil engineering and shore facility management programs. Cape May received the award again in 2011. The award is named in honor of Vice Adm. Kenneth C. Cowart (1905–1996), who served for more than 30 years in the Coast Guard, holding various engineering positions on Coast Guard vessels during World War II and then serving as engineer-in-chief from 1950 until his retirement in 1959. He received a Silver Star while serving as an engineer officer on the cutter *Campbell*, which suffered heavy damage on a convoy escort operation in the Atlantic on February 22, 1943.

In the early 1960s, the proposed training center expansion and development plan incorporated the concept of a new chapel. Between 1974 and 1976, a major effort was started for the planning and eventual construction of the new chapel. A fundraising drive was instituted, and over the years, about $29,000 was donated to help pay for its outfitting. In 1976, a project proposal for the new chapel was accepted by Coast Guard Headquarters, and in 1979, funds for its construction were approved by Congress. The building was designed by the Coast Guard Civil Engineering Design Branch, utilizing preliminary plans that were approved by the training center's Facilities Engineering Department. In September 1980, the construction contract was awarded to the A.J.J. Construction Company of Woodbury, New Jersey, and the new building was dedicated on May 6, 1982. Services were first held in the building several weeks before the dedication.

Three Sikorsky HH-52A Seaguard helicopters make their final flight out of Cape May on February 4, 1987, over Wildwood Crest, a barrier island community a few miles east of the US Coast Guard Training Center. This amphibious aircraft has been credited with saving 15,000 lives and $1.5 billion in property loss and damage since its deployment with the Coast Guard in 1963. It has the honor of having rescued more people than any other helicopter in the world and has become the international icon for rescue. With the advent of the HH-52A helicopter and additional air units, the sea-air rescue statistics for the Coast Guard increased dramatically. During the 10-year period from 1965 to 1975, the number of cases increased by 62 percent and the number of lives saved increased by 54 percent. The HH-52 was phased out of service after the HH-65A Dolphin entered Coast Guard service in November 1985.

In November 1984, one ammunition bunker was securely landlocked while the other had almost washed into the Atlantic Ocean. Two others, not seen in this photograph, were also on the beach by this time, all the subject of constant erosion from storms. The bunkers were erected during the World War II building campaign.

The rifle-firing range, seen here in 1984, has been at this location since at least the 1920s. With no development between the range and the ocean, the site was perfect for practice. Targets are set up in groups of four and an earth berm behind the range catches the spent bullets.

The Perfect Storm of 1991, also known as the Halloween Nor'easter, was one of the worst to hit the US Coast Guard Training Center in Cape May. Waves up to 30 feet high struck the coastline from Canada to Florida, causing extreme tidal flooding like that seen here along the harbor. Strong waves and persistent, intense winds caused extreme beach erosion—high tides along the shore in Cape May were only surpassed by the 1944 Great Atlantic hurricane. The Perfect Storm was a nor'easter that absorbed Hurricane Grace and later redeveloped into a small hurricane, killing 13. In the middle of the storm, the *Andrea Gail* sank, killing its crew of six and inspiring the book *The Perfect Storm*, which was later made into a movie. In the same storm, an Air National Guard helicopter ran out of fuel and crashed off the shore of New York's Long Island. Four members of its crew were rescued, and one was killed.

Seen berthed in front of the US Army *Quaker Hill* in this 1993 photograph is the US Coast Guard *Matinicus*, one of 49 island-class patrol boats, each 110 feet long, in the Coast Guard that were commissioned between 1985 and 1992. With excellent range and sea-keeping capabilities, this class is equipped with advanced electronics and navigation equipment. They concentrate on law enforcement—mainly drug and illegal-alien interdiction duties. Of the 49 built, 41 remain in service. All are named for United States islands and replaced the older 95-foot cape-class patrol boats. The *Matinicus* is currently stationed in San Juan, Puerto Rico, where it performs a variety of Coast Guard missions. A primary focus has been the interdiction of illegal immigrants seeking to enter the United States in small, un-seaworthy wooden boats called yolas. It also conducts drug smuggling patrols, undertakes fisheries law enforcement patrols, and is always on standby for search-and-rescue efforts.

Here, Coast Guard recruits learn how to extinguish a shipboard fire at the training center on September 11, 2007. Recruits practiced the procedure before donning fire protection gear and entering a completely dark and fog-filled room, which was their final test to complete basic firefighting training. (Courtesy of the US Coast Guard, PO2 Christopher D. McLaughlin.)

US Coast Guard PO1 Trisha Ortiz, a company commander at the US Coast Guard Training Center at Cape May, leads recruits through manual of arms training on January 5, 2012. Manual of arms is a uniform, close-order drill using weapons and is an important part of the recruits' military training. (Courtesy of the US Coast Guard, Chief Warrant Officer Donnie Brzuska.)

The US Coast Guard cutter *Dependable*, home-ported at the training center, is seen here after a change of command ceremony for the departing commanding officer, Comdr. George A. Lesher, and the new commanding officer, Comdr. David "Lee" Petty, on September 12, 2011. *Dependable* is a 210-foot medium-endurance cutter built at the American Shipbuilding Company in Lorain, Ohio, in 1968 and commissioned on November 22, 1968. For the next 23 years, it was stationed in Panama City, Florida, before moving to Galveston, Texas, in January 1992. It relocated to its current home in Cape May on August 4, 2000. Cutter 627, the *Vigorous*, is also home-ported at Cape May. A 210-foot cutter as well, it was originally commissioned in May 1969, and for nearly 23 years, was home-ported in New London, Connecticut. Throughout its 40 years of service, the *Vigorous* has enforced US fishery and immigration laws, interdicted illegal substances transported by sea, participated in search-and-rescue, and supported Homeland Security missions along the eastern seaboard. (Courtesy of the US Coast Guard, PO3 Cynthia Oldham.)

Capt. William G. Kelly (above, right) relieves Rear Adm. Cari B. Thomas of command of the US Coast Guard Training Center at Cape May during a change of command ceremony on June 23, 2010. Rear Adm. Timothy S. Sullivan (above, center), the commander of Force Readiness Command, gave remarks at the ceremony. Thomas graduated from the Coast Guard Academy in 1984 and served on three cutters, assisting in numerous hurricane responses, aircraft crashes, and oil spills. Her awards include five Meritorious Service Medals, a Joint Service Commendation Medal, and four Coast Guard Commendation Medals, among many other personal, unit, and campaign awards. She earned permanent cutter man status in 1994, and since July 2010, has been director of response policy. (Above, courtesy of the US Coast Guard, PO2 Christopher D. McLaughlin.)

The US Coast Guard Training Center at Cape May, seen here from the air in February 2012, has expanded greatly from its original size, when it was established as US Navy Section Base Nine in 1917. Very few World War I and World War II buildings remain, but those that do—like the commanding officer's quarters—continue to serve a useful function. Over 350 military and civilian personnel are attached to the training center. Many support services and resources are available to assist members and their families in handling professional and personal challenges. More than 4,000 of America's finest young men and women arrive for boot camp, the first chapter of their Coast Guard career. Also offered here are the Direct Entry Petty Officer Training Course, the Company Commander School, and the four-week Recruiter School. The sunset parades held three times each summer are open to the public and feature the recruit band, the drill team, and marching troops. (Courtesy of Richard Fedeke.)

BIBLIOGRAPHY

"The 75th Anniversary of Coast Guard Aviation." *Flightlines*. Summer 1991: 18–65.

Cook, W.G. "The Liberty Special." 1980.

Diemer, Joseph. "This Land of Ours: A History of the Training Center." *Cape May Eagle*, Vol. IX, Nos. 1 and 2: 18–31.

Dorwart, Jeffrey. *Cape May County, New Jersey: The Making of an American Seaside Resort Community*. New Brunswick, NJ: Rutgers University Press, 1993.

History of Cape May, NJ Section Base, U.S. Navy World War I, 25th Anniversary, 1942.

Hollemon, Kenneth. *From Whence We Came: A History of the Coast Guard in Southern New Jersey and Delaware*. Self-published, 1987.

Johnson, Robert Erwin. *Guardians of the Sea: History of the United States Coast Guard 1915 to Present*. Annapolis, MD: Naval Institute Press, 1987.

McCawley, E.L. *The War History of the Fourth Naval District from December 7, 1941*. 1945.

Scenes of General Activities at Camp Wissahickon. Brooklyn, NY: Albertype Company, 1918.

Scheina, Dr. Robert L. "A History of Coast Guard Aviation." *Commandant's Bulletin*, Issue 21-86, October 10, 1986: 9–43.

ABOUT THE
NAS WILDWOOD
AVIATION MUSEUM

The Naval Air Station Wildwood Foundation is a nonprofit organization whose mission is to restore Hangar No. 1 at the Cape May Airport in Cape May County, New Jersey, and to create an aviation museum honoring the 42 Navy airmen who died while training at the station during World War II.

In June 1997, NASW Foundation purchased Hangar No. 1 at the Cape May Airport. The 92,000-square-foot all-wooden structure was in a state of disrepair and required extensive renovation. Under the stewardship of NASW Foundation, the hangar was listed in the New Jersey and National Registers of Historic Places and is considered nationally significant for the role it played in World War II.

NAS Wildwood Aviation Museum now boasts over 26 aircraft displays as well as exhibits of military memorabilia, engines, photographs, and more. Additionally, the Franklin Institute of Philadelphia donated a wealth of interactive exhibits that allow visitors to discover the science of flight. The museum features a library, a food-vending area, and a recently expanded gift shop.

In its role as a community resource, NAS Wildwood Aviation Museum hosts activities, including fly-ins, aviation festivals, big band concerts, swing dances, veterans' ceremonies, historical lectures, school field trips, and senior tours. The museum is open daily during the spring, summer, and fall; please call for winter hours.

You are invited to become a member of NAS Wildwood Aviation Museum. Your membership supports the mission of the foundation, a tax-exempt 501 (c)(3) organization. Member are entitled to free admission to NAS Wildwood Aviation Museum, a 10-percent discount at the gift shop, advance invitations to special events and museum functions, reduced admission to special events, and issues of the aviation museum quarterly newsletter, the *Osprey*. Please help us give the past a future and become an NASW member.

Naval Air Station Wildwood Aviation Museum
500 Forrestal Rd.
Cape May Airport, NJ 08242
(609) 886-8787 • (609) 886-1942 (fax)
www.usnasw.org

DISCOVER THOUSANDS OF LOCAL HISTORY BOOKS FEATURING MILLIONS OF VINTAGE IMAGES

Arcadia Publishing, the leading local history publisher in the United States, is committed to making history accessible and meaningful through publishing books that celebrate and preserve the heritage of America's people and places.

Find more books like this at
www.arcadiapublishing.com

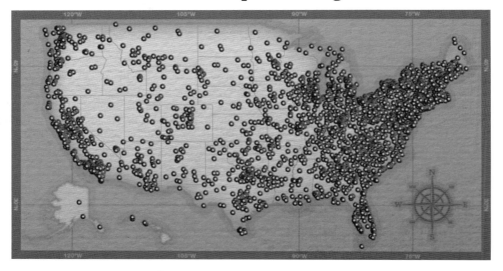

Search for your hometown history, your old stomping grounds, and even your favorite sports team.